WHAT MAKES
MEDICAL
TECHNOLOGY
SAFER?

KAREN LATCHANA KENNEY

LERNER PUBLICATIONS   **MINNEAPOLIS**

TO THE DOCTORS AND SCIENTISTS WHO PUSH THE LIMITS OF MEDICAL TECHNOLOGY AND KNOWLEDGE. THANK YOU FOR YOUR MANY DISCOVERIES!

Lerner Publications Company
A division of Lerner Publishing Group, Inc.
241 First Avenue North
Minneapolis, MN 55401 USA

For reading levels and more information, look up this title at www.lernerbooks.com.

Main body text set in Caecilia Com 55 Regular 11/16
Typeface provided by Linotype AG.

Library of Congress Cataloging-in-Publication Data

Kenney, Karen Latchana, author.
    What makes medical technology safer? / by Karen Latchana Kenney.
        pages cm. — (Engineering keeps us safe)
    Audience: Ages 9–12
    Audience: Grades 4 to 6
    Includes bibliographical references and index.
    ISBN 978-1-4677-7916-6 (lb : alk. paper) — ISBN 978-1-4677-8651-5 (eb pdf)
    1. Medical technology—Juvenile literature. 2. Biomedical engineering—Juvenile literature. 3. Medicine, Preventive—Juvenile literature. 4. Physical diagnosis—Juvenile literature. I. Title.
R855.4.K47 2016
610.28—dc23   2014046771

Manufactured in the United States of America
1 – VP – 7/15/15

CONTENTS

MEDICAL ENGINEERING

Some days, simply leaving your home can seem like a health hazard. Just listen to the news. Deadly viruses are spreading quickly. People are suffering from long-term health problems, such as obesity. The news travels fast too. With social media, you can hear about the latest health scare around the globe within minutes. It can be really alarming.

But listen a little longer and you'll also hear news about medical solutions. New ones are reported all the time. Some seem nearly impossible and are rare, like growing an ear on a patient's arm for transplant. Others happen on a regular basis. Surgeries reduce the size of people's stomachs to curb obesity. And disease detectives travel the world to find ways to stop the spread of dangerous diseases. Medical breakthroughs have already eliminated many major health risks. Countless diseases have now been cured or can be controlled.

So don't be afraid to step outside. Medical technology works to keep you healthy. With time and research, scientists find ways to cure or contain the latest health crisis. Their medical discoveries save millions of lives.

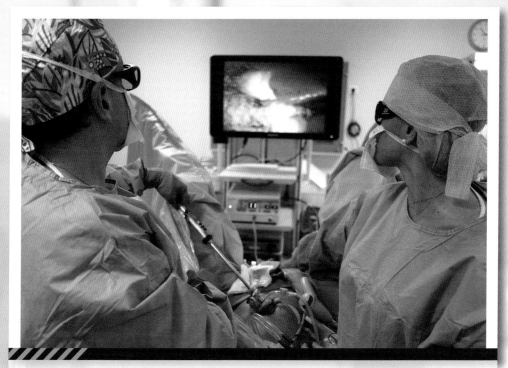

A medical team uses a 3-D camera to get a detailed view as they perform an operation.

BOOSTING DEFENSE

We're born with a system that's made just for our defense— our immune system. It's always on the lookout for invaders. When it finds a disease, it makes antibodies. They fight to destroy the disease before it spreads. But that system doesn't always work. Fortunately, scientists have figured out how to give it a boost.

Thanks to vaccines, your body can start fighting a disease before you even get it. A vaccine is a weak form of a disease. A vaccine is introduced into a person's bloodstream. The substance tricks the immune system into thinking you have a disease. White blood cells called macrophages absorb and digest the diseased microbes. But the macrophages keep the antigens. The antigens are the parts of the microbes that identify the disease.

Other white blood cells called lymphocytes recognize the antigens. Some lymphocytes latch onto cells infected by the disease and kill them with special chemicals. Other lymphocytes make antibodies—the immune system's secret weapon. Antibodies move through the bloodstream. They find hiding microbes and bind to them. The microbes cannot multiply. Soon microphages arrive to eat the microbes.

If you are healthy and don't have specific allergies, you don't get sick from the vaccine. But your body will have a memory of the disease's antibody. Your body knows how to instantly attack the disease if it should ever show up. This stops the disease from doing any harm.

Getting vaccinated protects you from many different diseases.

STOPPING SMALLPOX: EDWARD JENNER

In the eighteenth century, smallpox killed hundreds of thousands of people. Edward Jenner, a British doctor, experimented with cowpox, a similar disease, to see if it could be used to protect people from smallpox. In 1796, Jenner rubbed material from a person's cowpox sore into a scratch on a boy's arm. The boy became sick but recovered. A few months later, Jenner transferred some material from a smallpox sore into the boy. The boy did not get sick. By 1800, Jenner's new vaccine was being used throughout England and in many other parts of Europe.

DISEASE DETECTIVES

Diseases can spread quickly, especially if a person is sick and does not know it. Just touching an infected person's skin or being exposed to a sneeze or a cough might transfer certain diseases. To stop the spread of a disease, people need to know how the disease works. That makes it easier to find, monitor, and treat victims. It also helps protect others from infection.

It's a disease detective's job to understand how deadly diseases spread. Disease detectives in the United States work for the Centers for Disease Control and Prevention (CDC). Once an outbreak is discovered, the CDC sends its detectives to the site of the outbreak. Each disease needs to be handled differently.

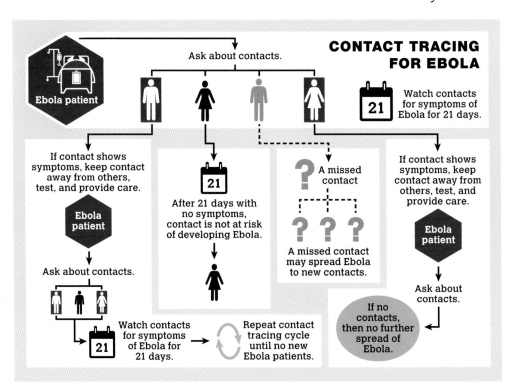

CONTACT TRACING FOR EBOLA

Ebola patient

Ask about contacts.

Watch contacts for symptoms of Ebola for 21 days. **21**

If contact shows symptoms, keep contact away from others, test, and provide care.

Ebola patient

Ask about contacts.

Watch contacts for symptoms of Ebola for 21 days. **21**

After 21 days with no symptoms, contact is not at risk of developing Ebola. **21**

A missed contact

A missed contact may spread Ebola to new contacts.

If contact shows symptoms, keep contact away from others, test, and provide care.

Ebola patient

Ask about contacts.

Repeat contact tracing cycle until no new Ebola patients.

If no contacts, then no further spread of Ebola.

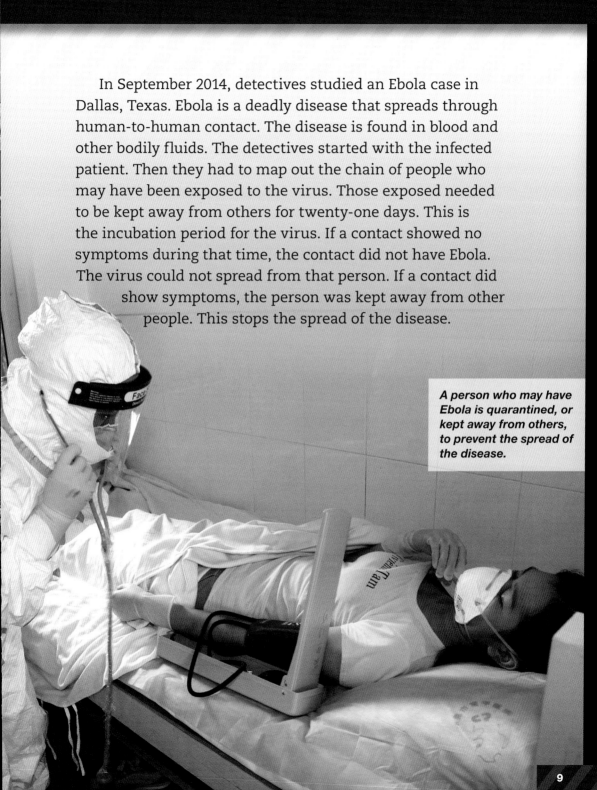

In September 2014, detectives studied an Ebola case in Dallas, Texas. Ebola is a deadly disease that spreads through human-to-human contact. The disease is found in blood and other bodily fluids. The detectives started with the infected patient. Then they had to map out the chain of people who may have been exposed to the virus. Those exposed needed to be kept away from others for twenty-one days. This is the incubation period for the virus. If a contact showed no symptoms during that time, the contact did not have Ebola. The virus could not spread from that person. If a contact did show symptoms, the person was kept away from other people. This stops the spread of the disease.

A person who may have Ebola is quarantined, or kept away from others, to prevent the spread of the disease.

IT'S IN THE GENES!

Everything that makes us unique—from our hair color to our potential health issues—is found in our genes. Within each cell of our bodies are pairs of DNA (deoxyribonucleic acid). The DNA contains chemical codes that determine our traits.

Genes are segments of DNA. These genes are passed down to us from our parents. Some diseases or risk factors that can lead to diseases are passed down through families. Until the late twentieth century, people didn't know what was in their genes. Genetic testing changed that.

To perform genetic testing, a health-care worker takes a sample of hair, blood, skin, or other tissue, or the fluid around a fetus in the womb. These samples all contain cells loaded with DNA and genes. The samples are sent to a laboratory. Technicians search the genes for indications of certain diseases. They look for parts of genes that are missing, duplicated, or altered. They also look for genes that are not active or too active. The results tell patients if they carry genes that make them at risk for developing diseases. This often gives patients time to try to reduce that risk through medical treatments or changed habits before they get sick.

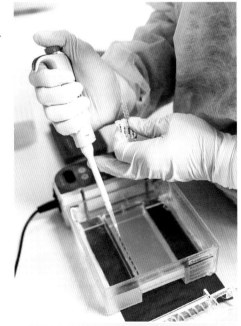

A researcher applies genetic material to a gel for DNA testing.

AN IMPORTANT 1 PERCENT!

Humans have between twenty thousand and twenty-five thousand genes in each cell. Most of these genes are the same in every human being. Just 1 percent of our genes determine our unique physical traits.

DNA DOUBLE HELIX

Strands:
- phosphate
- sugar

Base pairs:
- adenine
- thymine
- cytosine
- guanine

- hydrogen bond

strands

A scientist examines the results of a patient's genetic test.

MRI: A 3-D VIEW

If you have health problems, a look inside your body can reveal a lot about them. This look is often essential for a diagnosis. But how can you see inside without surgery? One way is through magnetic resonance imaging (MRI). This technology can produce images of almost anything inside the human body. This includes internal organs, the spinal cord, and the brain. The MRI creates these images by relying on the magnetic properties found inside our cells.

About 60 percent of the human body is made up of water. Water molecules contain hydrogen and oxygen atoms. Inside the hydrogen atoms are protons. The tiny protons act like magnets inside the body. Each has an axis that is very sensitive to magnetic fields. The axis has two poles, just like Earth. Each proton spins on its axis. Normally, the protons spin and do not align inside the body. These tiny proton magnets are the focus of an MRI machine.

The MRI machine consists of a large tube that contains strong magnets. A patient lies on a bed that moves through the tube. When exposed to the MRI's magnetic field, all the hydrogen protons in the patient's body line up. Their axes point in the same direction. Then the scanner sends radio waves to certain parts of the body. The waves make the protons in that spot fall out of alignment. When the waves are turned off, the protons start to align again. As they do this, they send radio waves back to the machine. A receiver in the machine maps out these signals to make a detailed image of the body part. The images can be 3-D, showing highly accurate views of the body.

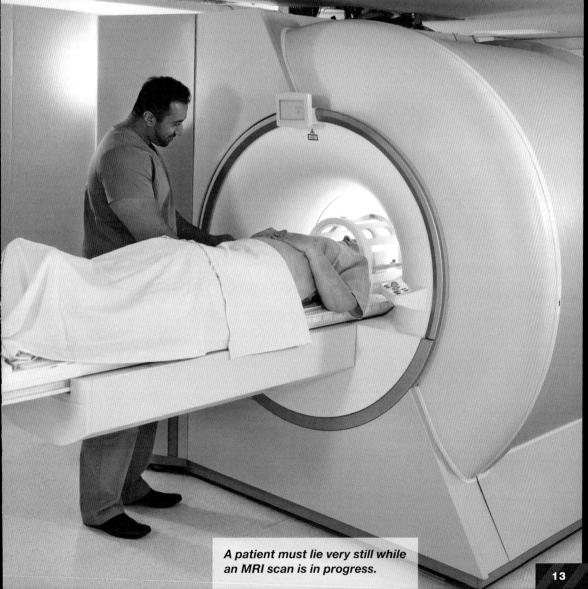

NOBEL WINNERS

MRI technology is so important to the medical field that it has been recognized with a Nobel Prize. In 2003, scientists Paul C. Lauterbur and Peter Mansfield were awarded the Nobel Prize in Physiology or Medicine. These two scientists developed ways to pinpoint certain areas of the body and create fast and precise images using MRI technology.

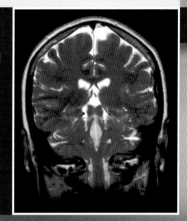

A patient must lie very still while an MRI scan is in progress.

BLOOD FLOW IN ACTION

A superhighway runs through your entire body. Your circulatory system allows oxygen-rich blood to flow to your many cells. This system is long too. If your blood vessels were laid out in one line, it would stretch more than 60,000 miles (96,560 kilometers)! At the hub of this highway is the heart. It pumps the blood in a one-way direction through the body.

Blood needs a clear route to get to all parts of the body. But over many years, a waxy substance called plaque can build up inside the blood vessels. Plaque can come from eating too many foods high in cholesterol. When plaque hardens, it narrows blood vessels and limits the amount of blood that can flow through. Eventually, a blood vessel can become completely blocked. A heart attack occurs when blood is cut off from the heart. That's why it is important to know how well blood is flowing through the blood vessels.

A coronary angiography is a test that shows blood flow. First, a thin tube is placed in a person's blood vessel by the groin or the inner crease of the elbow. The tube is threaded through the vessels until it reaches an area that needs to be studied. Then a

The circulatory system is made up of the heart, arteries (in red), veins (in blue), and capillaries.

special dye is released into the bloodstream. The dye is pumped through blood vessels by the heart. This dye, containing iodine, can be seen with an X-ray machine. Normally, blood vessels do not show up on X-rays. But the iodine makes them visible. The X-ray machine quickly takes a series of images. They reveal how the blood flows through the blood vessels. The images show plaque buildup and potential blockages.

SYNTHETIC INSULIN: ENERGY KEYS

Do you know how the energy locked inside food gets into our bodies? When food reaches our digestive system, it is broken down into glucose, a form of sugar. The glucose is then released into the bloodstream. From there, glucose searches for cells in need of energy. But it can't get inside those cells without insulin. Insulin opens cell doors to let the needed glucose inside.

This isn't so easy for people with diabetes. The pancreas, which makes insulin, either stops making it, doesn't make enough, or makes insulin that does not work right. Glucose fills the bloodstream, unable to get into cells. The cells do not get enough energy to work well. The body tries to rid itself of the glucose through urine. A person with diabetes feels tired and loses weight. He or she is thirsty and hungry all the time and has circulation and vision problems. Untreated diabetes can lead to foot or leg amputation and blindness. There is no cure for diabetes. But synthetic insulin makes it possible to live with the disease.

Scientists have created a way to grow insulin in a laboratory. They alter a type of bacteria so that it produces insulin. This insulin is identical to the insulin made inside a human. It exists in a liquid form that is injected into

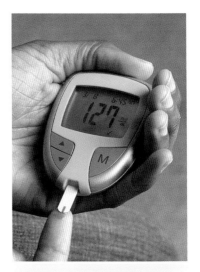

Many people with diabetes test their blood sugar with a blood sugar meter.

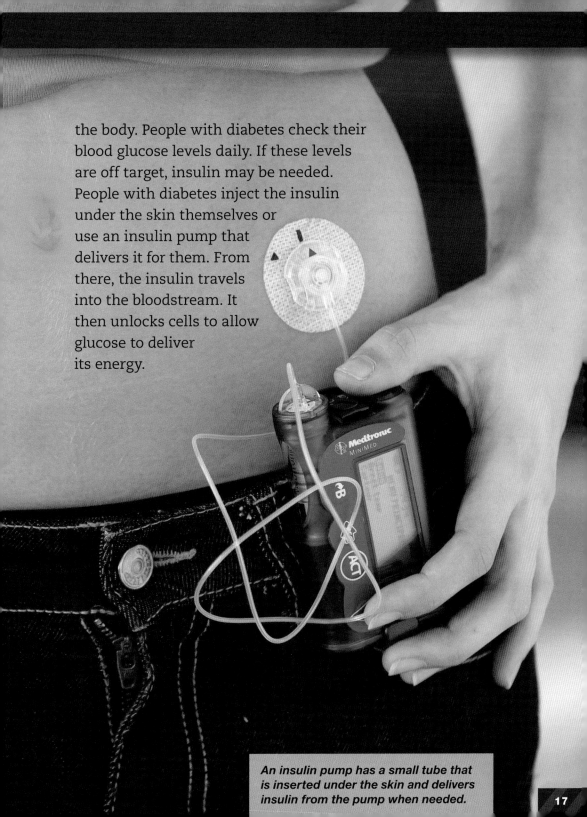

the body. People with diabetes check their blood glucose levels daily. If these levels are off target, insulin may be needed. People with diabetes inject the insulin under the skin themselves or use an insulin pump that delivers it for them. From there, the insulin travels into the bloodstream. It then unlocks cells to allow glucose to deliver its energy.

An insulin pump has a small tube that is inserted under the skin and delivers insulin from the pump when needed.

TACKLING OBESITY: BARIATRIC SURGERY

Obesity is a major problem in the modern world. Compared to previous centuries, many people lead less active lifestyles and eat more processed foods that are packed with calories. One way to measure obesity is through body mass index (BMI). This is a measure of a person's body fat based on height and weight. Normal BMI ranges from 18.5 to 24.9. People who are severely obese have a BMI of 40 or higher.

For people who are severely obese, diet and exercise may not be enough to lose weight. Bariatric surgery, or gastric bypass, is another option for these people. It restricts the amount of food a person's stomach can hold. It also limits the amount of food absorbed by the body.

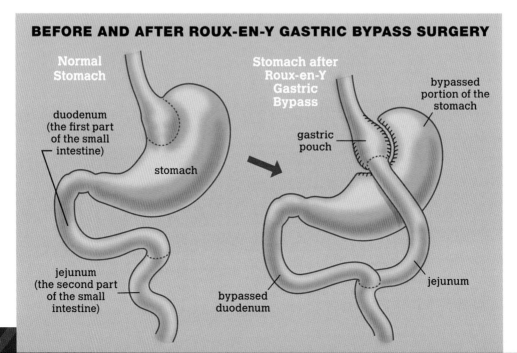

BEFORE AND AFTER ROUX-EN-Y GASTRIC BYPASS SURGERY

Normal Stomach

duodenum (the first part of the small intestine)

stomach

jejunum (the second part of the small intestine)

Stomach after Roux-en-Y Gastric Bypass

bypassed portion of the stomach

gastric pouch

bypassed duodenum

jejunum

The Roux-en-Y is a common type of bariatric surgery in the United States. During this surgery, a surgeon turns a small part of a person's stomach into a pouch roughly the size of an egg. Food will go directly into this pouch instead of into the rest of the stomach. This also limits the amount of food a person can eat at one time. The new stomach pouch is connected to the middle section of the small intestine. The small intestine is where most of the calories and nutrition are absorbed from food. Food then avoids much of the small intestine so fewer calories are absorbed into the body. People who are severely obese can lose around half their weight after this surgery over the course of months and years.

In addition to exercise and healthful eating, gastric bypass surgery can be an effective treatment for obesity.

FIGHTING CANCER: CHEMOTHERAPY

Our bodies are filled with billions of cells. When something is wrong with a cell, it divides to make two new cells. This replaces the damaged cell. But cancer cells divide and multiply at very fast rates. They form masses, or tumors, in the body.

Chemotherapy drugs kill cells by damaging cell parts and making the cells unable to divide. But chemotherapy also damages cells in the body as they divide. Cancer cells rapidly divide, so they are the most affected by the drugs. Most healthy cells in an adult are not usually dividing, so they are less likely to be damaged. But some healthy cells are constantly dividing. These cells, including hair cells, bone marrow cells, and skin cells, can be harmed by chemotherapy. This is why a person's hair falls out during chemotherapy. (These side effects do not last after chemotherapy is finished.)

Once the cancer cells are killed or stopped from dividing, chemotherapy can end. Healthy cells can then start dividing to replace

CELL DIVISION

Cell

nucleus

chromosomes made of genes

Cell makes exact copies of its genes.

Cell starts dividing.

Two new cells are made. Each has a complete set of genes.

cells killed or damaged during the treatment. The cancer patient then goes into remission. A full remission means the cancer can no longer be found in the body. A partial remission means the cancer is still in the body but is no longer growing.

Chemotherapy is often delivered to a patient through a tube placed in a vein.

MUSTARD GAS

A poisonous gas first used during World War I (1914–1918) was the first clue in the development of chemotherapy. When used as a weapon, the gas causes blisters on the skin and mucus membranes, such as the lining inside the nose or on the eyes. The US Army studied how the gas affected people exposed to it during the war. They noticed that it slowed cancer growth in the lymph nodes. Mustard gas became a model for cancer-fighting drugs. Drugs similar to the gas were developed that damage the DNA of certain cancer cells, killing them.

COMPUTER GLASSES: SURGICAL ASSISTANCE

With new technology, medical procedures are becoming more and more effective. Some surgeons have started using Google Glass during their surgeries. Google Glass can record a person's point of view, connect to the Internet, live stream, and display images. It is becoming a useful tool in surgeries. It helps surgeons perform better and record their surgeries for teaching purposes. And it allows them to view X-rays or medical history exactly when it is needed. This can help surgeons make critical decisions quickly.

Cancer surgeons can use the gadget to assist them when removing tumors inside organs. Usually X-rays show the exact location of tumors that need to be removed. These X-rays must be viewed on a machine away from the patient—so the surgeon's focus on the patient while operating is broken. With the computerized glasses, the surgeon can load the X-rays into the technology. A small portion of the surgeon's view then includes the display. The surgeon can slightly shift focus to review the X-rays when needed. The surgeon can continue operating without ever turning away from the patient and the operating table.

Hospitals continue to find new ways to use computerized glasses. A paramedic at the scene of an accident can wear the glasses. A doctor in an emergency room can view the patient at the scene through the paramedic's glasses. The doctor can then offer lifesaving advice before the patient even reaches the hospital.

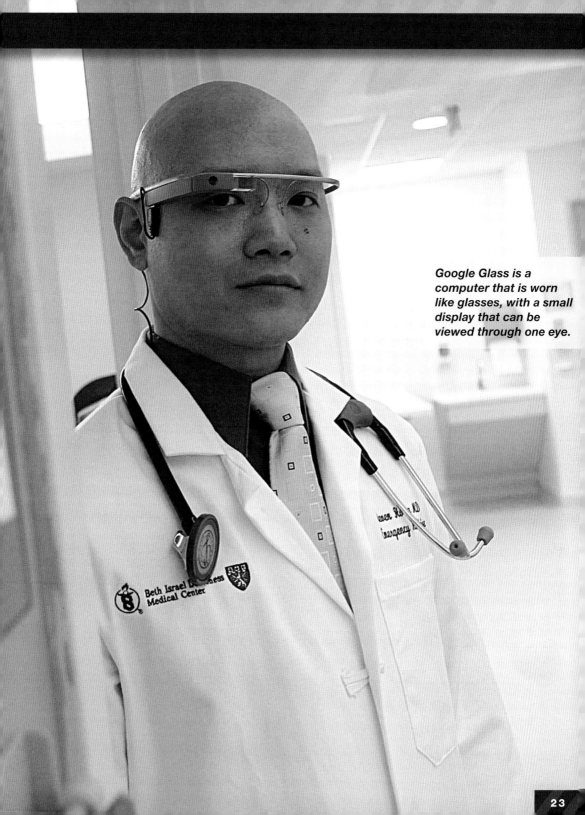

Google Glass is a computer that is worn like glasses, with a small display that can be viewed through one eye.

BODY PARTS ON DEMAND

Transplants are risky surgeries. When a patient receives a replacement organ, such as a heart or an eye, from someone else, the patient's body can get confused. The body sees this new organ as an invader and sometimes attacks and destroys that organ. And that's not the only tricky part of the process. It can take years to find a matching donor for a patient. Patients need organ donors with the same blood type and same tissue type.

To sidestep these challenges, scientists are beginning to grow body parts from a patient's cells. Simpler parts, such as bladders, have been grown in laboratories. This technology is still in the development stage. Yet scientists are working toward growing more complex organs, such as hearts.

To grow an organ, scientists first need to grow cells. They choose the correct type of cell from the patient. They mix the cells with a growth material in a laboratory. The cells rapidly multiply. Next, scientists create a mold for the cells to form around. The mold will hold the shape of the organ or the tissue being grown. The mold is made of material that the body will accept. Once inside the body, the mold will break down so that only the grown tissue is left.

A scientist covers a mold of an ear with stem cells.

The mold is covered with the cells grown in the laboratory. They continue to grow around the mold. The new organ or tissue is kept in an incubator. This machine keeps the new organ or tissue warm and moist. The cells bond together to form the organ or the tissue. When finished growing, the new organ is transplanted into the patient.

This synthetic ear will break down in the body once new cells have grown around it.

PRINTING ORGANS

It sounds unreal, but printing organs may someday be commonplace. Scientists at the Wake Forest Institute for Regenerative Medicine have modified ink-jet printing technology to print fully formed, functional organs and tissue. Skin cells and materials to help them survive and grow are placed in a printer cartridge. The cells can then be "printed" directly onto patients' bodies. However, this type of therapy is not yet available to patients, and it may be some time before it is.

STEM CELLS: UNLIMITED POTENTIAL

Stem cells are unlike any other cells in the body. These cells can come from very early embryos or the fluid surrounding babies in the womb. They can also come from umbilical cords or adult tissues. Stem cells can do more than simply divide to make identical copies of themselves. They can create other kinds of specialized cells found in the body. This capability is very exciting to researchers.

Since the 1970s, stem cells have been used in the treatment of leukemia. This form of cancer attacks the tissues that produce blood, such as bone marrow. Once a patient has leukemia, the bone marrow and the white blood cells are destroyed during chemotherapy and radiation treatments. The patient is then injected with healthy stem cells. The stem cells travel through the bloodstream and enter the bone marrow. Inside, the stem cells start dividing to create healthy white blood cells.

Stem cells may prove useful to medicine in many other ways. Scientists are trying to see if stem cells can help grow new heart tissue in damaged hearts. Some human trials show that stem cells do help repair heart tissue. Stem cell use has great medical promise. But more research is needed to unlock its full potential.

Drops of stem cells line this dish in a laboratory.

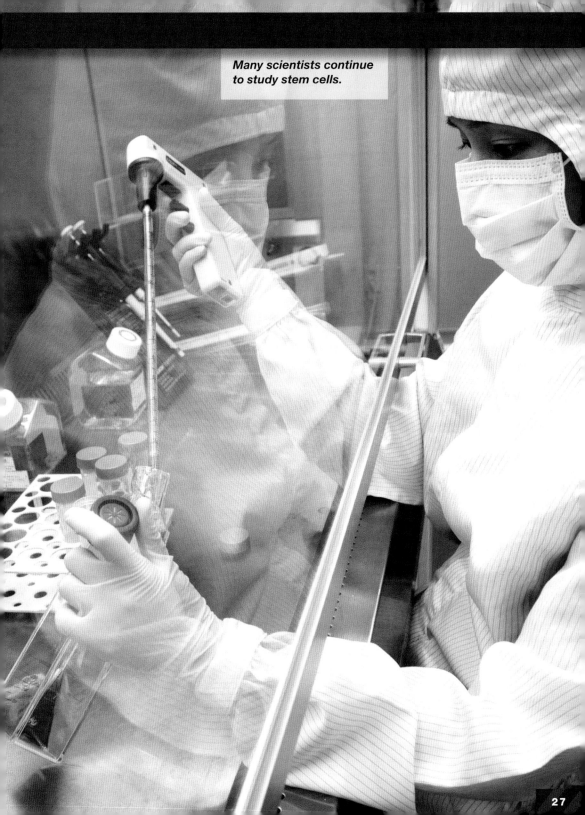

Many scientists continue to study stem cells.

THE POWER OF MEDICINE

Every year, new medical solutions solve health issues.
Some health problems virtually disappear thanks to medical technology. Illnesses that once wiped out entire cities can now be completely avoided through vaccines. Health problems such as diabetes can be managed with medicine. Genetic testing lets people know if they are at risk for diseases so they can better manage and treat them. And dangerous diseases can be better understood through the research of disease detectives. Much more is waiting to be discovered in the field of medicine. And new technological breakthroughs may be just around the corner.

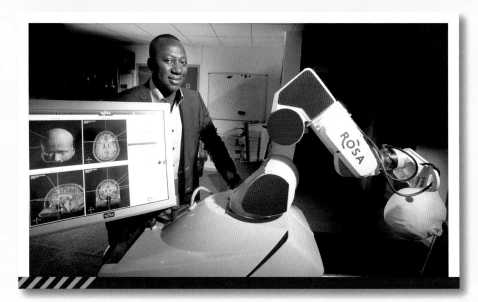

Bertin Nahum invented Rosa, a robot that helps surgeons perform brain surgery in hospitals around the world.

GLOSSARY

antibody: a protein that is made in the body and that attacks diseases and viruses

bloodstream: blood that circulates through the body

diagnosis: a medical professional's conclusion about what disease or health problem a patient has

duplicate: to make a perfect copy of something, such as a cell

microbe: a germ or organism that is too small to be seen by the human eye and must be viewed under a microscope

molecule: the smallest part of a substance that contains all the properties of that substance

outbreak: a sudden start of something, such as a disease

proton: a small part within the nucleus of a cell

radiation: the sending out of rays or particles of energy to treat diseases

synthetic: manufactured by humans rather than found in nature

virus: a tiny organism that can reproduce and grow only when inside a living cell

SELECTED BIBLIOGRAPHY

Champeau, Rachel. "UCLA Physicians Use Google Glass to Teach Surgery Abroad." *UCLA Newsroom.* June 11, 2014. http://newsroom.ucla.edu/stories /ucla-physicians-use-google-glass-to-teach-surgery-abroad.

"How Chemotherapy Works." Cancer Research UK. Accessed November 17, 2014. http://www.cancerresearchuk.org/about-cancer/cancers-in-general /treatment/chemotherapy/about/how-chemotherapy-works.

"How Is Genetic Testing Done?" *Genetics Home Reference.* Accessed November 17, 2014. http://ghr.nlm.nih.gov/handbook/testing/procedure.

"The Nobel Prize in Physiology or Medicine 2003." Press release. Nobelprize. org. October 6, 2003. http://www.nobelprize.org/nobel_prizes/medicine /laureates/2003/press.html.

"Obesity and Overweight." World Health Organization. January 2015. Accessed November 17, 2014. http://www.who.int/mediacentre/factsheets/ fs311/en/.

Philbin, Tom. *The 100 Greatest Inventions of All Time: A Ranking Past and Present.* New York: Citadel, 2003.

Riedel, Stefan. "Edward Jenner and the History of Smallpox and Vaccination." *BUMC Proceedings* 18, no. 1 (January 2005): 21–25. Accessed November 17, 2014. http://www.ncbi.nlm.nih.gov/pmc/articles/PMC1200696/.

"Tests and Procedures: Coronary Angiogram." Mayo Clinic. Accessed November 11, 2014. http://www.mayoclinic.org/tests-procedures/coronary -angiogram/basics/definition/prc-20014391.

Vogel, Gretchen. "Organs Made to Order." *Smithsonian Magazine,* August 2010. Accessed November 17, 2014. http://www.smithsonianmag.com/40th -anniversary/organs-made-to-order-863675/?no-ist.

FURTHER INFORMATION

Ballen, Karen Gunnison. *Seven Wonders of Medicine*. Minneapolis: Twenty-First Century Books, 2010. Learn about the advances in medical technology from the past to the present.

Bryant, Jill. *Medical Inventions: The Best of Health*. New York: Crabtree, 2014. Read about the many inventions that have helped advance the field of medicine.

The Diabetic Dog Game
http://www.nobelprize.org/educational/medicine/insulin/game/insulin.html
Play this game to see what is needed to keep someone with diabetes balanced and feeling well.

Getting an MRI
http://kidshealth.org/kid/closet/movies/video_mri.html
Visit this site to watch a video that shows what it is like to get an MRI.

Go, Go Stem Cells
http://learn.genetics.utah.edu/content/stemcells/sctypes/
Learn more about stem cells and where they are found in the body.

Jacobson, Ryan. *Marvelous Medical Inventions*. Minneapolis: Lerner Publications, 2014. Discover the strange stories behind some of medicine's greatest inventions.

Learn the Facts
http://www.letsmove.gov/learn-facts/epidemic-childhood-obesity
Learn the facts about childhood obesity and why exercising and a good diet are so important.

INDEX

PHOTO ACKNOWLEDGMENTS

The images in this book are used with the permission of: © nevodka/Shutterstock.com, p. 1; © iStockphoto.com/Sproetniek, p. 5 (lab background); © Boris Horvat/AFP/Getty Images, p. 5 (doctors with 3-D camera); © MediaforMedical/Jean-Paul Chassenet/Alamy, p. 7 (teen girl); © Everett Collection Inc/Alamy, p. 7 (Edward Jenner); © Laura Westlund/Independent Picture Service, pp. 8, 11 (DNA diagram),18, 20; © ChinaFotoPress/Getty Images, p. 9; © Philippe Garo/Science Source, p. 10; © Rafe Swan/Cultura/Getty Images, p. 11 (genetic researcher); © Guy Croft SciTech/Alamy, p. 13 (MRI scan); © Hero Images Inc./Alamy, p. 13 (MRI machine); © Leonello Calvetti/Alamy, p. 14; © Zephyr/Science Source, p. 15; © Mark Hatfield/Getty Images, p. 16; © RGB Ventures/SuperStock/Alamy, p. 17; © Zoonar GmbH/Alamy, p. 19; © Miodrag Gajic/Vetta/Getty Images, p. 21; © Suzanne Kreiter/The Boston Globe via Getty Images, p. 23; © Matt Dunham/AP/CORBIS, pp. 24, 25; © Mauricio Lima/AFP/Getty Images, p. 26; © Jo Yong-Hak/Reuters/CORBIS, p. 27; © Patrick Aventurier/Getty Images, p. 28.

Front cover: EPA/Marcial Guillen/Newscom.